Celebrating Our Holidays

Celebrating HANUKKAH

By Elizabeth Morgan and
Arlene Erlbach

Cavendish Square
New York

Published in 2023 by Cavendish Square Publishing, LLC
29 E. 21st Street New York, NY 10010

Website: cavendishsq.com

Library of Congress Cataloging-in-Publication Data

Names: Morgan, Elizabeth, 1993- author. | Erlbach, Arlene, author.
Title: Celebrating Hanukkah / Elizabeth Morgan, Arlene Erlbach.
Description: New York : Cavendish Square Publishing, 2023. | Series: Celebrating our holidays | Includes index.
Identifiers: LCCN 2021039988 | ISBN 9781502664822 (library binding) | ISBN 9781502664808 (paperback) | ISBN 9781502664815 (set) | ISBN 9781502664839 (ebook)
Subjects: LCSH: Hanukkah–Juvenile literature.
Classification: LCC BM695.H3 M673 2023 | DDC 296.4/35–dc23
LC record available at https://lccn.loc.gov/2021039988

Editor: Katie Kawa
Copyeditor: Jill Keppeler
Designer: Deanna Paternostro

The photographs in this book are used by permission and through the courtesy of: Cover pp. 1, 4 Africa Studio/Shutterstock.com; back cover, pp. 3, 5, 7, 9, 11, 13, 15, 19, 20, 23, 27, 28, 29, 30, 31, 32 N.D.Vector/Shutterstock.com; pp. 6, 18, 21 ChameleonsEye/Shutterstock.com; p. 8 Anna Kraynova/Shutterstock.com; p. 10 lev radin/Shutterstock.com; p. 11 Nick Brundle Photography/Shutterstock.com; p. 12 LevT/Shutterstock.com; p. 14 P Maxwell Photography/Shutterstock.com; p. 16 Nicku/Shutterstock.com; p. 20 Noam Armonn/Shutterstock.com; p. 22 Golden Pixels LLC/Shutterstock.com; p. 24 Derek Hatfield/Shutterstock.com; p. 25 Olaf Speier/Shutterstock.com; p. 26 Pixel-Shot/Shutterstock.com; p. 28 (marshmallows) gresei/Shutterstock.com; p. 28 (chocolate) Dan Kosmayer/Shutterstock.com; p. 29 (pretzel sticks) Tiger Images/Shutterstock.com.

CPSIA compliance information: Batch #CSCSQ23: For further information contact Cavendish Square Publishing LLC, New York, New York, at 1-877-980-4450.

Printed in the United States of America

CONTENTS

Hanukkah is sometimes called the Festival of Lights. A festival is a time to celebrate.

CHAPTER ONE

EIGHT NIGHTS OF CELEBRATING

Some holidays are celebrated on one day every year. Others have celebrations that last longer. One of these holidays is Hanukkah, which lasts for eight days and nights. Hanukkah is a special holiday for Jewish people around the world. It begins on the 25th day of the Hebrew, or Jewish, month called Kislev. This is in either November or December on the Western calendar that's used in many places around the world, including the United States. Hanukkah is a celebration of light, and it's a hopeful and happy time for all who honor it.

LIGHT IN THE DARKNESS

Hanukkah is one of the most well-known Jewish holidays. Even people who aren't Jewish are familiar with one of the most important **symbols** of Hanukkah: the candleholder with nine candles. Many people call this candleholder simply a "menorah." However, the correct name for the candleholder Jewish people use during this time of year is a *hanukkiah*. It's also known as a Hanukkah menorah, which is different from any other kind of menorah.

A hanukkiah is a kind of menorah, or Jewish candleholder, but not every menorah is a hanukkiah.

On each night of Hanukkah, families burn candles in this candleholder. They also often exchange gifts, eat special foods, and attend parties. Singing songs and playing games are fun Hanukkah activities too.

The Jewish People

"Hanukkah" is a Hebrew word. Hebrew is the language of the Jewish people, also known as the Jews. They're a group connected by a shared culture, or way of life, and religion. They even have their own calendar. Many Jewish people live in the nation of Israel, which is a place deeply connected to Jewish history. However, many others live in other countries around the world, including the United States.

The History of Hanukkah

Hanukkah is often celebrated around the same time that Christians celebrate Christmas. In fact, some families celebrate both holidays. However, Hanukkah and Christmas celebrate different events. Christmas celebrates the birth of Jesus Christ—the most important figure in the Christian religion, or belief system. Hanukkah gives thanks for a battle that the Jewish people won more than 2,000 years ago against the Seleucid Empire, which had its roots in ancient Greece. The king who ruled over the Jews at the time told them that they couldn't practice their religion. They weren't allowed to pray in the main Temple, their place of worship.

After winning their fight with the empire, the Jewish people took back the Temple. Then, they **rededicated** it to God. The word "Hanukkah" means "dedication" in Hebrew, and this holiday celebrates the dedication of what's known as the Second Temple. Understanding the history of this holiday—and of the Jewish people as a whole—is an important part of celebrating it.

Judaism has been practiced for thousands of years, and it's still one of the world's major religions.

CHAPTER TWO

WHO CELEBRATES HANUKKAH?

Jewish people around the world celebrate Hanukkah. The religion they practice is called Judaism, and it's one of the oldest religions in the world. The Jewish people have faced many hard times throughout their history, and Hanukkah is a celebration of an important victory during one of those hard times.

THE HISTORY OF JUDAISM

Judaism is an ancient religion. Jewish people believe in one god. They also tell stories of important people in the history of their faith. A man named Abraham is considered the father of the Jewish people. Moses is another well-known Jewish person. It's said that God gave him the 10 Commandments, which are rules for people to follow to live a good and holy life. Other important figures in Jewish history included prophets, who told people what God wanted them to do, and kings, who led the Jewish people.

The stories of these leaders and other important aspects, or parts, of Judaism are found in the Tanakh—the Hebrew Bible. Jewish people today are led by teachers called rabbis. They call the places where they pray synagogues.

Some people call a Jewish place of worship a temple. However, others believe there was only one temple—the Temple of Jerusalem, which was destroyed between 587 and 586 BCE. When it was rebuilt, it was called the Second Temple, but that was destroyed in 70 CE.

Following the Rules

Judaism has certain rules for its followers. Some Jewish people are **stricter** about following these rules than others. For example, some Jewish people follow certain rules about what they can and can't eat. These people don't eat pork or shellfish. They eat only food that's kosher. This means the food has been prepared in a certain way.

Jewish people observe their Sabbath, or holy day, from Friday at sundown until Saturday at sundown every week. Many Jews celebrate the Sabbath, which they call Shabbat, in their home with a special meal. They may also go to their local synagogue for prayer services. Some Jews don't work, drive cars, use electricity, or spend money during the Sabbath. This time is meant to be a day of rest and prayer, and keeping it holy is one of the 10 Commandments.

Hope in Hard Times

Hanukkah honors a major Jewish victory over people who tried to **oppress** them. However, this was not the only time the Jewish people have come under attack. More than 3,000 years ago, the Egyptians enslaved the Jewish people. The spring holiday of Passover celebrates the end of this period of

Orthodox Judaism

There are different branches, or kinds, of Judaism practiced around the world. Orthodox Jews follow a very strict branch of their religion. They closely follow the rules for what they can and can't eat, which are also known as dietary laws. They also say daily prayers and dress in a modest way. This often includes head coverings. In addition, men and women are separated in the synagogue for Orthodox religious services.

enslavement. In modern times, German Nazis killed more than 6 million Jews throughout Europe during World War II (1939–1945). This period of suffering and death is known as the Holocaust.

Although powerful groups have tried to destroy them throughout history, the Jewish people have continued to spread their faith around the world. Hanukkah is a time to celebrate the ways the Jewish people have kept their faith alive in hard times and to remember to hold on to hope in moments of darkness.

There are around 14 million Jewish people living all over the world today, including in the Jewish nation of Israel, which is shown here.

Shown here is a Hanukkah menorah at the Western Wall—also known as the Wailing Wall. It's one of the last remaining pieces of the Second Temple left standing in Jerusalem, Israel, today. The Second Temple plays an important part in the story of Hanukkah.

CHAPTER THREE

A Miracle for the Maccabees

The story of Hanukkah begins with the Second Temple, which was located in Jerusalem—the holiest city in Judaism. The Temple was the religious center for the Jewish people. They would visit the Temple and pray. In the Temple, there was a special oil lamp that was always kept lit. It was used to light all the other sacred lights there.

Priests were the men who took care of the Temple. They made sure this lamp—the "eternal light"—never went out. They kept the lamp filled with special oil that they made from olives. It took more than a week to make the oil, and no other oil could be used.

Many different groups controlled the lands around the Temple throughout history. Hanukkah calls back to a time when the Seleucid Empire ruled over these lands and the Jewish people.

The Greek Way of Life

Around 330 BCE, a ruler named Alexander the Great took control of Palestine—the land the Jewish people lived on. He brought with him the religious beliefs of the Greek people, which were different from those of the Jews. The Greeks

Many synagogues today have their own eternal lights to honor the one that burned in the Temple of Jerusalem thousands of years ago. That ancient light was lit using oil kept in a jug similar to this one.

believed that many gods controlled the world. Even though the Greeks had different religious beliefs, they generally let the Jews pray in peace.

However, in 175 BCE, a new king, Antiochus IV, began ruling Palestine as part of the Seleucid Empire. He told the Jews they had to give up their religion and become like the Greeks in every way.

The new king wouldn't allow Jewish religious services to be held. He destroyed religious objects in the Temple. He replaced them with statues of Greek gods. He ordered the Jews to pray to these statues. If the Jews refused, they would be killed or enslaved.

The Maccabees Fight Back

During the reign of Antiochus IV, a priest named Mattathias lived in a village outside Jerusalem called Modi'in (sometimes spelled Modein). In 167 BCE, some of the king's soldiers came to the village. They tried to get the villagers to offer a sacrifice to a Greek god. However, Mattathias stayed true to his religion and refused.

One man offered to do what the soldiers wanted. Mattathias then killed that man and the leader who'd told them to make the sacrifice. Later, Mattathias, his five sons, and other Jews in the village left to hide in the mountains. Sometimes they came down from the mountains to attack the king's men. Many Jewish people joined with Mattathias and his men. They'd started a rebellion, or an uprising.

The rebellion lasted for about two years. Mattathias died during the first year. Before his death, his son Judah took over. Judah and his men kept fighting even when things looked hopeless. They continued to hammer away at their enemy. They became known as the Maccabees.

What's a Miracle?

Hanukkah celebrates a moment that Jewish people consider to be a miracle. A miracle is something good that happens that's unexpected and can't be explained, so people often say God made it happen. People who follow many different religions believe in miracles and say they still happen today. For example, if someone is very sick but gets better even though their doctors can't explain how, their family might call that a miracle.

Shown here is Mattathias gathering Jewish men to his cause.

This is because Maccabee comes from the Hebrew word for "hammer." Their uprising is now known as the Maccabean Revolt.

The Miracle of the Maccabees

The king's army was much larger than the forces of the Maccabees. Its soldiers also had better weapons. However, Judah Maccabee was a great leader. He and his soldiers believed that God would help them win.

The Maccabees won three battles against the king's troops. The king thought he would finally win if he led a fourth battle. He got together thousands of soldiers, but the Maccabees won again. Then, the Maccabees marched to Jerusalem to fix the **damage** that was done to the Temple.

Judah Maccabee and his men removed the statues of the Greek gods from the Temple. They cleaned off dirt and blood that was on the walls. Then, Judah went to light the "eternal light." It's said that Judah found only enough oil for the light to last for one day. It would take longer than that to make more oil. By what appeared to be a miracle, the oil lasted for all eight days until more could be made. Judah was able to prepare more oil so the lamp wouldn't go out again. This was a reason to celebrate!

Judah Maccabee had started a new holiday for the Jewish people. It would be celebrated every year and would last for eight days and nights. This holiday is called Hanukkah, and it celebrates the miracle of the Maccabees.

The Hanukkah menorah is the most famous and sacred symbol of Hanukkah. It's often proudly displayed in Jewish homes throughout the eight nights of this holiday.

CHAPTER FOUR

THE MOST IMPORTANT SYMBOL

Hanukkah celebrates the eight nights the oil lasted to keep the "eternal light" in the Temple lit. This is why the holiday lasts for eight nights. It's also why there are eight smaller candles on the Hanukkah menorah. This is the most important symbol of Hanukkah, and the **traditions** and rules around it carry special meaning for the Jewish people.

A CLOSER LOOK AT THE CANDLES

Lighting the Hanukkah menorah is a way for Jewish people to feel connected to the story of the Maccabees. A Hanukkah menorah contains nine candleholders. One of the holders is for the candle known as the shammash (sometimes spelled shamash). "Shammash" means "helper" in Hebrew. This is the candle that's used to light the other eight candles.

The other candles stand for each night of the miracle of the oil. On the first night, the shammash is used to light one candle. On the second night, the shammash is used to light two candles. On the third night, three candles are lit with the shammash. The lighting of one more candle each night goes on until all of the candles are lit on the last night. This is the most sacred way the Jewish people honor this Festival of Lights.

The shammash is often raised above the other candles in a Hanukkah menorah. It's the only candle that can be used to light the other candles.

Hanukkah Menorah How-To

The lighting of the Hanukkah menorah is a tradition that's been carried out for centuries, and there are certain rules to follow to do it correctly. On the first night of Hanukkah, a candle is placed in the holder farthest to the right and is lit with the shammash. Each night, another candle is placed in the Hanukkah menorah and lit. The candles are always added from right to left and lit from left to right, so the newest candle is lit first.

Special prayers are said each night as well. The prayers said during the eight nights of Hanukkah praise God and also express thanks for the miracles the holiday celebrates. These prayers, which are also called

Respecting All Holidays

Hanukkah is celebrated around the same time as Christmas, Kwanzaa, and other winter holidays celebrated by different groups. It's important to show respect toward people who celebrate different holidays and to make them feel comfortable during this festive time of year. This is why many people say "Happy Holidays!" in December. This is a way to wish people happiness no matter what holiday they celebrate.

In some parts of the world, Jewish communities celebrate Hanukkah with a public Hanukkah menorah display.

blessings, are generally offered in Hebrew. They're also often sung instead of said.

The candles in the Hanukkah menorah should be allowed to burn for at least half an hour. Hanukkah candles are special and should be used only in the Hanukkah menorah.

Many families put their Hanukkah menorah near a window for everyone to see. In many families, people take turns lighting the candles. In other families, each person has their own Hanukkah menorah. The lighting of the Hanukkah menorah is an important tradition for family members to share together. It brings them closer during this special time.

Families and friends sometimes gather together for Hanukkah parties where they exchange gifts and play games.

CHAPTER FIVE

GIFTS, GAMES, AND GOOD FOOD

Lighting the Hanukkah menorah is the most sacred part of Hanukkah, but it's not the only way people celebrate this important holiday. They give gifts, eat traditional foods, and play games on these eight special nights. It's a joyful time of year, and Hanukkah celebrations are often fun and festive!

GELT AND OTHER GIFTS

Gifts have become a big part of Hanukkah for many Jewish families. However, giving gifts wasn't originally part of Hanukkah celebrations. Over the years, the tradition of giving gifts began, but the ways Hanukkah gifts are exchanged and the kinds of gifts that are given differ from family to family.

Some children receive gifts on each of the eight nights of Hanukkah. Other families give gifts to each other on only one night of the holiday. Many children are given gelt, or money, as a Hanukkah gift. However, for some families, Hanukkah is a time to give gifts or money to those who are less fortunate instead. Gifts can be a fun part of the holiday, but the reasons to celebrate go much deeper than presents.

Chocolate coins are a popular Hanukkah gift. They look like real gelt, but they're actually a tasty treat!

Special Foods

Like many holidays, Hanukkah has special foods that families eat and serve at parties. Latkes, or potato pancakes, are a common food on Hanukkah dinner tables. The latkes are fried in oil as a way of remembering the oil from the Temple in Jerusalem. Some families eat jelly doughnuts called *sufganiyot*. These, too, are fried in oil.

Applesauce is another popular Hanukkah food. It's often served with latkes. Sometimes sour cream is served with latkes too.

In addition, Hanukkah cookies and other sweet treats that aren't fried in oil have become a part of the holiday celebrations in many Jewish households. These cookies are often decorated with symbols of the holiday, including the Hanukkah menorah.

Hanukkah celebrations often feature good food, such as applesauce.

How to Play a Hanukkah Game

Another symbol of Hanukkah is the dreidel. It's is a toy that looks like a spinning top with four sides. A different Hebrew letter is printed on each side. These letters are: nun, gimel, he, and shin. They stand for a Hebrew phrase that means, "A great miracle happened here."

Each letter also stands for an activity in the game that's played using the dreidel.

Different families have different ways of playing dreidel. Many people begin the game by putting a coin, nut, or piece of candy in the center of an imaginary circle. Then, each player takes a turn spinning the dreidel. Depending on which letter the dreidel lands on, the spinner

Dreidel is a fun game for people of all ages.

"The Dreidel Song"

Unlike Christmas, which has many songs written about it, Hanukkah doesn't have a lot of songs. However, a popular song about this holiday is called "I Have a Little Dreidel," but it's also known simply as "The Dreidel Song." It's a song about playing with a dreidel, and it begins, "I have a little dreidel. I made it out of clay. And when it's dry and ready, then dreidel I shall play."

either takes everything in the center, adds one piece to the center, takes half of what is in the center, or does nothing. A player is out of the game when they have to put something into the center but have nothing left to use. The winner is the person who has collected everything from the center.

Lighting the Way

Playing dreidel, eating latkes, and opening presents are fun parts of Hanukkah. However, they're not the most important parts. The lighting of the Hanukkah menorah is at the center of this holiday. Hanukkah happens during a time of year when the days are short and nights are long in the Northern **Hemisphere**. Lighting the Hanukkah menorah is a special way to brighten up the darkness of winter and to honor the hope that light brings in dark times. The Festival of Lights is a hopeful holiday, and it's a time to celebrate with family, friends, and faith.

Make a Marshmallow Dreidel

Ingredients:

1 can vanilla frosting

12 pretzel sticks

12 large marshmallows

12 Hershey's Kisses or similarly shaped candy

blue and silver decorating sugar

Shown here are the basic parts of a marshmallow dreidel: the candies, marshmallows, and pretzels.

DIRECTIONS:

1. Press one pretzel into one marshmallow, leaving some of the pretzel sticking out of the top.
2. Cover the marshmallow with a thin layer of frosting, and roll it in the decorating sugar so the whole surface is covered.
3. Use a small dab of frosting to "glue" the flat end of the candy to the end of the marshmallow opposite the pretzel.
4. Repeat the first three steps with the remaining marshmallows and pretzels.
5. Let the marshmallow dreidels stand for at least 30 minutes to let the frosting "glue" set.

GLOSSARY

damage: Loss or harm done to a person or piece of property.

hemisphere: Half of Earth.

oppress: To control or rule in a harsh or cruel way.

rededicate: To dedicate—to officially make something a place for honoring a person or event—again.

strict: Carefully following the rules, especially of a belief system.

symbol: Something that stands for something else.

tradition: A way of thinking, behaving, or doing something that's been used by people in a particular society for a long time.

FIND OUT MORE

Books

Bullard, Lisa. *My Family Celebrates Hanukkah*. Minneapolis, MN: Lerner Publications, 2019.

Lindeen, Mary. *Hanukkah*. Chicago, IL: Norwood House Press, 2019.

Markovics, Pearl. *Hanukkah*. Minneapolis, MN: Bearport Publishing, 2019.

Websites

Hanukkah Facts for Kids
www.dkfindout.com/us/more-find-out/festivals-and-holidays/hanukkah/
This part of the DK Find Out website explains important parts of Hanukkah, including the Hanukkah menorah and the dreidel.

***National Geographic Kids*: Hanukkah**
kids.nationalgeographic.com/celebrations/article/Hanukkah
Visitors to this website can read a short article and watch a video about Hanukkah.

Publisher's note to educators and parents: Our editors have carefully reviewed these websites to ensure that they are suitable for students. Many websites change frequently, however, and we cannot guarantee that a site's future contents will continue to meet our high standards of quality and educational value. Be advised that students should be closely supervised whenever they access the Internet.

INDEX